TIPPOO SULTAN'S INCREDIBLE WHITE-MAN-EATING
TIGER TOY-MACHINE!!!

Tippoo Sultan's Incredible White-Man-Eating Tiger Toy-Machine!!!

DALJIT NAGRA

faber and faber

First published in 2011
by Faber and Faber Ltd
Bloomsbury House
74–77 Great Russell Street
London WC1B 3DA
This paperback edition first published in 2012

Typeset by Faber and Faber Ltd
Printed in England by T. J. International Ltd, Padstow, Cornwall

A CIP record for this book
is available from the British Library

ISBN 978–0–571–26491–9

2 4 6 8 10 9 7 5 3 1

I dedicate my roaring verse to Katherine
Though it seems with rosy breath she faked
My hand to tame the lines that lie herein
Like Tippoo's roar that lies in the V&A!

Acknowledgements

Earlier versions of poems appeared in the following publications: *Channel 4 at 25*, *Guardian*, *London Review of Books*, *Manhattan Review*, *Matter*, *New Yorker*, *The North*, *Observer*, *Poetry London*, *Poetry Review*, *Reactions* and *Times Literary Supplement*.

The author is gratified by the serendipity permitting him to pounce upon the following: Flora Annie Steel's version of *Bopoluchi* ('A Ballad for Bopoluchi'), Rudyard Kipling's *Lispeth* ('The Legend of Lispeth') and Elizabeth Sarah Mazuchelli's *The Indian Alps And How We Crossed Them* ('The Ascent of a Victorian Woman').

This book was improved by Matthew Hollis, Stephen Knight and Katherine Hoyle. Additional support was provided by Archana Rao and Kuldip Sodera. I am grateful to Charles Beckett for supporting my application for an Arts Council England grant, to JFS School for being so accommodating. I'm also indebted to my favourite comic duo: Maia and Hannah!

Contents

TIPPOO SULTAN'S INCREDIBLE WHITE-MAN-EATING
TIGER TOY-MACHINE!!!

The Balcony Song of Raju & Jaswinder

RAJU

. . . won't you come downstairs I'm caught in the rain
and I'll stay here all day with my box of matyai
though your mum might be shocked by this shoe-caste boy
who squats in her oak by her bright golden gates.

JASWINDER

Go away dirty boy, yoo is bad bad lover
we danced in di car to Bally Sagoo
on di way from Henley to Sutton Hoo
and I luv it up di flumes ov di Alton Tower!

Vut a summer it was when yoo teach me to kiss
or to walk wid yor hand and not blush in public,
den I hear how yoo bin through di ladies
like a rickshaw round New Delhi!

RAJU

Well it's true I went round the block with Bulwinder
                         I went with Kuswinder
                         I went with Subwinder
          I even went to the mela with Ramwinder!

But their skirts were too short
and they loved their alcopops
they all chewed gum
and they swore too much
so none of these girls made me feel right inside.

Then one day standing out of the temple
the one to turn me fundamental
her hair was beehive'd
in a honey-coloured sari
it doesn't take much to realise
it was you Jaswinder – you're my Bollywood hotty!
Even though you're the star of the landowner caste
only you take me back to my past.

JASWINDER

Yoo is cute, such a cute, such a cute cute lad
but yoo act wid no bezti. And here in di West
can we be all one caste? If I speak to my dad
he may fast get me feathered in di uncle's nest
                in Baluchistan or in Pakistan
                in Hindustan or in No-Woman-Staan!?

RAJU

I regret my name was the cause of sharam
my honour is lost, I'm as foul as a harem,
a moral for randy young bloods
who go hot off the press when their fun is undone.

I regret getting stuck in the thickets with Mukjit
                getting locked in the wicket with Jamjit
                running up burns on the benches with Scarjit
                being stung pulling thorns out of Bungjit.

So no more Puldeep or Sagdeep or Bagdeep
and no more Lukveer and no more Hotveer
only one name is true and it's my Jaswinder!

JASWINDER

Vut a summer it was in di heights
ov di moors and di Scafell Pike
and we rolled through di flowers
and we hugged in di bowers.

Vut a summer it was when at night off di road
we would sleep wid di cows in a field
or we played wid di lambs and di goats
and di farmers said *ai!* we could milk deir sheep.

Den one night it appear dat di lion ov yor Leo
he was pouncing his stars at di wings of my Virgo,
on di ground in a queue were di black-bright eyes
ov di cows and di goats and di sheep and di lambs,
den we saw we were caught in a tight crop-circle,
di snort ov a pig only stop when we huff off di land!

RAJU

Oh Jaswinder, even though you're the star
of the landowner caste
only you take me back to my past.
I must live with that morning in Hampton Court
when you led me by the hand to the heart
of the maze and you sat us on the floor
and you picked up a leaf and you said we'd gone too far
and we stayed in the deep trying to murder our names
and I'll wait for you there in the heart of the maze.

The Gob-Smacking Taste of Mine Inheritance!

Where's the taste
Of mine inheritance?
– GEORGE HERBERT, 'The Bunch of Grapes'

That Brit, they say, felt pressed
  by the call to race & save
    his flag of vintage glory,

so he raised a purple bruise
  & a sour tang on the tongue
    of a Punjab shop-wallah.

That Punjab, they say, then tried
  to instil this taste in his kids
    for he'd age here, rootless.

What a common tale man must pass on
  to man: this battle for turf,
    when we've been forged by the Crown.

When Her stall was set out abroad
  & franchised the English line
    that binds my rights, as a native poet,

to graft my heathen-Word on our old soil.
  Henceforth the stock of the store
    is the fruit of a mutual realm!

Phallacy

How oft do mates bang on at length about
the length they're hung and grab their crotch to slash
the air then chuck an arm at will around
a chum while necking Stella till they're lashed.
To tell the truth, I'm really not well hung,
and thus I hide from mates my prince's state,
this conk is king of my poor frame, no trunks
would lunchbox find to bank a lady's gaze.
And yet I hope the guys won't feel too down
when I recount my lover's hardly wimpish –
watch her stiffen over *corrrrrs!* from louts
who check her out too long (for she's that fit!).
    In bed, most nights she'll sigh: *O love, I love
    the woman's way you work your subtle touch.*

The 13 O'Clock News

Pip Pip, today's feature for Monarchy Month is the first
Indian knighted, in 1842. His name is Sahib Sir Jamsetjee
Jeejeebhoy. But why was a Queen keen to knight a native?

The answer lies with the man in a red 'phone-box',
the Arch Liberator, the Truth-Sleuth, you know him
as every lady's Tonk-Honker: Johhhn Simpsonian!!!

O John Simpsonian, do you ZoomBoom for us?
Pip Pip . . . our connection is scrambling . . . I'll be brief . . .
This self-made good chap had a chequered mid-life . . .

It seems that in Opium Wartime Jeejeebhoy ran
the speediest clippers bound for China . . . As you see,
I've landed at the port . . . at the Yangtze gorge . . .

Those hordes of mango wood boxes are Jamsetjee's . . .
And the men with machetes are unloading each box
with brown balls inside as big as a comely lady's breast . . .

O John Simpsonian, through gyres and galaxies,
you're the boldest ZoomBoomer! *If I may sum up,*
in this dim droopy night . . . the love-sick mass of men

lined along the bank . . . as though a whole nation
of John Chinamen and Shangrilanders sleepwalking
for a toke, a cut, a suck of the dream of empire . . .

Tippoo Sultan's Incredible White-Man-Eating Tiger Toy-Machine!!!

To flesh a career
in poems you rifle
through your stash
of coolly imperial
diction. Dying
to blood that hoard
swotted since foreign
kid of the class
who chewed the fat
of the raw meat minty
tongue that English
is
nowadays your wrought
state. You're awfully
scary once in your
stripes! You claw
at the mirror – overcome
by the camps of history!
Thus
when that top-hat sahib
screams, O God
your eyes are ablaze
observing themselves
in the cull you're
no longer mankind
once you're the Sher
of Punjaaab on the wallahs of the

rrrrraaaaaaaaaaaaaajjj!!!

Our Daughter, the Bible Flasher!

. . . but you must our daughta cure Dr Jekly!
Spells by wife is mek daughter worse.
I tell of how it start: at party for full moon
di girls is whooping wid broomstick dance
and wise-hair ladies gassing voodoo-powders
in corner. I leav di Bacardi guggling
Bernand-Manning-to-Edingborough-Duke
joke-cracking boys who mek di *haha! ah?*
In hallway I see a girl twitchey her nose.
O Dr Jekly, it our Rapinder, her sari –
tutt-tutt-tuttering to lino!
                              Underneath
she hav white collar and black costume!
Wid eyes to ceiling artex, wid bible she march
for marquee, screeching like dis (I sing):
All tings briiiiight and beauuuuuti-
pelll, di God-lord changing allllll . . .
Such jumble, Dr Jekly, she mumbo, so quick
up I roll her to play wid Black Magic masks
in attic. And ask, *Vut is wrong wid Rub?*
Always, again in British on me:
Does he too do Christmas making money
for charities with Cliff Richard?

The Ascent of a Victorian Woman
from a journal

To see Darjeeling and die!
To witness the mountains pronged to the heavens
And reside in a temperate clime.
Though the trek to our cross on the mount
Is a damper The Chaplain opines:
'The journey's the thing!'

While the train may have crossed the alpine peaks,
At our staging post, once past the cupolas and domes
Of Calcutta, past the deadly swamps, the morass and fens
Of the Hooghly (a region as though of Atlantis
With merely the tips of palm trees peeking through)
We are met by our somewhat pallid driver:
'Wid di most compounded respect, Madams,
Meet Di GBT.' 'The what?' I ask.
'Madam, di carriage comparable to a summer's day:
Di Goverrment Bullock Train!'
Said with exuberant pride that even the 'D'
Of his 'The' seems capitalised.

How the Hindu, who was once the cradle of civilisation,
Has fallen into parody,
For our driver directs us to a 'hackery'
Furnished with a rough tilt
And yoked by two scrawny bullocks.
Then tousling his whiskers he points at The Chaplain:
'Madam, is dat most excelling person wid you also lady?'
I'm forced to exclaim: 'That is my husband!'
By and by, the Chaplain unravels from blankets

To reveal his unmistakably mannish boot.
His 'Why you brute!' meets a flurry of 'Sorry, Sahib'.

. . .

Our driver makes no apology for not greasing
The wheels of squeaking solid wood.
He sits proudly astride a pole and flogs the bullocks.
My pleas for mercy lead him to twirl their tails
With lashings of *Bettychudes* and *Banchudes*
(Apparently from a lexicon of expletives).

He provokes no response from the natives
Lying shrivelled on their charpoys
Beneath what pass for trees. What pass for bees
Seem asleep on the wild flowers
With no hurry for honey.
                      The rooks too
Seem possessed by the climate and do not whirl
About the elms. A butterfly seems to pass the day
Folded on a harebell stalk, and a screech from a bird
Passes by unrequited over the sinister two-bodied gaur.

The Chaplain groans with a migraine
As if his heart from the journey's bosom
Had absented from the outset. When asked of our
Whereabouts, our driver, who's perpetually lunged
Into the style of a jockey, asserts:
'Sahib, our petty pace is far from di Grand Trunk Road,
Any more I can no frognosticate.'
The delivery of our Shakespeare-wallah
Remains unnerving. He has the patter of a baboo
Who works for a Public Works Department.

In any case he leads us where humanity
Has entirely receded along the narrowest breadth
Of harsh white phantom ground for the fulsome flat-land days
And dusty miles. For we seem no closer
To our real ascent, and with the thermometer
Standing at anything you care to mention.

Gunga Jumna

you know that day when it comes
all your family are gathered at the flight path
to welcome you home
you are asked to touch the feet of your
hunch-back great-grandmother which you do
but then she lifts you up on a cackle
and puts around your head a haar

in a clay back-room your gaze
is drawn to gods on juggernauts
battling about the egg of the earth
on a hand-woven drape
which you sense is over a telly

when the khaki and ochre unformed
gourds are skonked on the hearth
singing women blade large lumps
for the evening stew

as you know by now the electricity goes
and every villager is around a fire
with ancestral tales
of tales from around the ancestral fire
whilst gaurs and frogs are woken
by the far-off yawp of a calf
being born or swallowed by a snake

The Monsoon Song of Raja Narcissus

all the girls say they love me
all their mums say i'm lovely
ever since i lived in the clouds

ever since you left
i've been raining on the road
where you first said you loved me

This Be the Pukka Verse

Ah the Raj! Our mother-incarnate
Victoria Imperatrix rules the sceptred
sphere overseeing legions of maidens'
'fishing fleets' that break the waves
to net the love of a heaven Etonian!
Fetes on lawns with mansion whacking
banks or dances by moonlight
at the Viceroy – the Viceroy's ball!

The barrack room burra pegs
of brandy pawnee and pink gin
and toddy to doolally flappings
on *Jaaaldi punkawallaaaahh!*
for six meal days including tiffin
with humps and peacock and tongue.
The lock, stock and bobbing palanquins
for summers on gothic verandahs

where dawn Himalayas through Poobong
or Ooty mist for housey-housey
and hammocks under the Milky Way.
Tally ho! in topi-of-khaki
with swagger stick for bobbery
shikars, and by Amritsar what a
12-bore Hollis howdah from howdahs
bang! bang! bagging photogenic

tigers! Panthers, leopards, blackbucks
and bustards. And Kipling or Tatler
to hand at Tollygunge. The rum twirling
sabre-curved mustachios lavish
zenanas behind bazaars with a fruity
hookah for the breathless nautch,
the nautch that leads to ayahs
and passer-by *goodies* snookered

for sahibs sport that ends
in the hushed-up bezti births
of half-breed bastards growing up
cursed as mad dogs and vagabonds
in a jolly good lingam-land overflowing
with Hobson-Jobsons of Holi,
and opium and silk and spice
and all the gems of the shafted earth!

Raju t'Wonder Dog!

First good penny I spent in 'uddersfield,
after t'shop, were on a sweet-as-ladoos
alsatian, against me wife, Sapna's wishes.
Reet from t'off there were grief cos Beena,
what's Sapna's friend, were visitin' –
showin' off her reet bonny aubergine sari
t'spit o' Meera Syal. Appen t'cage fer Raju
weren't locked . . . I were fettlin' stuff
on t'other aisle when I 'eard him skatin'
towards t'till fer Beena! I legged it to

'ead him off, 'cept I forgot about me new
pink wafer display – all t'tower, as I
lunged round t'corner, kem crashin'!
I lay ont' floor watchin' Raju anglin'
fer a kiss – Beena's mouth gaped wide
as t'Pennine Tunnel; a bob-haired lass went:
Tha gret wazzock! Rolled ont' floor
near me wi' laffin', got me laffin' too
and t'queue of 'ouse weefs near weein'.

Our Sapna could strangle that daft mutt
what's narked our few relations from visitin'
'cept Raju helps us deal wi' sorrows:
all t' 'arf-price 55lb sacks o' tatties
sold in t'world won't buy us a little 'un.
And t'IVFs keep failin'. She'll be seen
as havin' dodgy karma by t'community
fer 'er past-life sins made 'er barren.

From time ter time she'll say: *Get thee sen*
a fresh bride who'll production line
fer you an heir! Who'll get our 'ard earned
dosh, eh? Raju?
       By t'way 'soofna' means 'dream' –
a bit like Sapna in't it? That's why Raju
and me'll stoop and I'll say: *Sapna,*
you're me soofna. Why would I do
owt like to upset me soofna? Chucklin'
she'll add: *Aah Avtar, you're me avatar.*
T'customers'll coo or look reet confused.

In t'storeroom, as Raju kneels like 'e
were in t'temple, Sapna'll say that even if
t'price hungry customers turn their backs
cos they've bin teken by t'bright lights
o'Morrisons, we'll never be left looking
at our sens warped in t'shopliftin' mirrors
cashin' up at night wi' nowt in t'till
fer we've got Raju! And mebbe he's secretly
t'incarnation of some 'indu God ovvaseein'
we don't wake from t'fate of our soofna.

Transport for Londonstan

That's not tlc. I tease snuffling from the sofa.
That finger around my head – it's more like TfL.

You jump in saying, *Tlc should be bodies*
goo'd together under the same shell.
And there you have me cos I too
can be a snail-commuter and not very on-time
when you need a cuddle.

Are we become Captain Spocks in our super-vacuum'd
Starship home, or have we sold our souls to
Health & Safety in our Domestos obsession with the lav?

For the Special Fare Day, you reckon, we'll be hand-in-hand
on the Waltzer armchair of a tunk-tunk-tunkety
train that ptoooouums off its tracks

and wafts us out for the bumper clouds

from where we'll fling our Oyster Cards over Bognor
roaring our raspberry heads with

MMIIINNDD
       THE
              GGGGGGAAAAAAPPPPPP!!!

Singh in School

EK) THE TURBANATOR WHIP HAND!

Sunday mornings kneeling at the gurdwara . . .
Then lungar & gawping at the golden rows of paintings
where Moghul blades slavered with blood
over our headless saints (whose haloes shone overhead).

Those glorified losses got updated
by our school's first ever turbanated Sikh.

I joined the rest at the balcony
when NFs at lunch, to check him out,
slopped his cream turban & soaked him up
for monkey blood! When drained he somehow swung

& swung & swung till a Skin who'd seen enough
knelt & pieced him back his immortal pound of flesh.

Our civilising school trip was to *Annie*
where my safest English courts a girl,
at once I get my mum's imprint: *Gori?*
The verdict rubs her chalk-face down in dirt!

O mum, one caste I get: gori. She balls
my world. Her sky-eyes cage me on to fours:
O mum, just watch her spot these jungly arms,
so aren't these long-haired hairy fingers claws?

We're one mothered earth and yet, O mum,
I spear me for the laws of tidal-blood!

Once at the show, her locks are close to hand,
they're breathing haloes – how they summer turfs
in me to mound upon our kingdom-sand,
unnationed!
                    O mum, how island of me I'm . . .

TEN) KABBA BARES HIS CHEST BEFORE MR BULRAM AT
      THE CONSTIPATIONAL REARING OF HIS WARRIOR SON!!!

So his lunch getting spent in detention vid stool for his butt?
Do u vunt him to tink dat our caste made for butt-lickey work!?
Get him wrestling at lunch so he learn cad-cunnery to flirt
vid a boy, who he drop like a damson to kiss in di dust!

Dat is vy afta school he's in jockstrap to beat our guerillas
at press-ups & sit-ups & squat-ups, from park he returns –
I him time in di bath so he catch from di tub all my chickens!
So my boy to join tum-head-toe-nail-belly-back surgeon wallahs?

Ah so Bulram ju vunt us to brown-nose as old-fogeydonian?
He new breed ov John Bull! His guts are so tough vid fresh parts:
ven he filmed to dive he vil mooney deir script! Like deir Raj
come to end so my boy in di ring who is dumping, as dooshman,

on his butt Big Daddy as granny handbags hit di shame
ov dis Shirley. Vee no more seen as di hole for deir buttom!

CHAR) THE FAIR ISSUE SITS THE ETON ENTRANCE
       EXAMINATION

Hopscotching, or hoofing a ball down the hawthorn lanes,
or blaring their whoops on strawberry chews, the boys
couldn't care how you follow your father beyond the gates

where swans on the banks are a-flap for the touristy shoots
and boys in canoes are in tune to the count from a tannoy,
you stumble behind your father on cobbled routes

whose head follows men in gowns stamping the ground,
you float through weeping willows of breeze till the fields
spire shadows and throw you wide open out . . .

You return past gargoyles, past the ball-hoofing boys,
to be dark as the darkest lobby where you're relieved
you stand in a corner. Your father's cardamom voice

echoes on stones and tells you how your brother
will follow in the footsteps of maharajas!

PUNJ) SCHOOL DAZE WOZ THE BEST DAZE!?

O wot fun we had we roamed savannah
damp-rooms propped wiv gum to do our time
thru chalked-up sawdust hours wiv spanners & hammers
or needle-&-thread to mesh the head of a tiger.
Thrown out at break we'd pea-shooter nails at yids
& monkeys & gingas & gyppos wiv Puma Trainers,
chuckin' a javelin at a metal-legged flid!
Then pigged on soggy fat-chips & more spam fritters,
wiv sauce for blood & blottoed on coke, our farts
around the library gassed Ms Owl! Then we fed
our books to dogs! Then we stoned them Panda cars!
Stormin' alleys, lovin' it! livin' it! gettin' 'ead!

Urgh you dirty starin' day-trip sonnet tossers!!!
Is this some feedin' time behind zoo-bars!??

A Ballad for Bopoluchi

Hauling pails from the village well
the girls fell a-talking of weddings to come.
Said one, *My uncle will bring me chum-chums.*
Said a second, *My uncle will bear me gilded
satin saris.* The third, Bopoluchi, the fairest
and fastest of the lot, *My uncle, with caskets
of jewels and fruits on a luscious white horse
will ride us to his palace to win me a suitor!*

Poor Bopoluchi, the orphan, knew no uncle
to manicure her caste in the matter of marriage;
instead at the well from where he sold his wares,
a robber's heart roly-poly'd for her wild cat eyes,
and hungered for a virginal feast. On a horse
at dawn beside Bopoluchi's hut he pronounced
he was her father's brother. He bore caskets
of jewels – he was just what she'd prophesied!

As they galloped along Bandicoot Lane, she nuzzled
her cheek in his chest as he claimed a noble past.
But a crow on a branch viciously croaked:
*Oh Bopoluchi, have you lost your headdd?
This hot-head thief will cut off your neckkk!*
Uncle, said Bopoluchi, *that crow sounds anxious.*
Pooh, said the robber, *the crows in this country,
that peacock, that jackal are like niggling wives!*

In a room with a thousand rowdy jewels
the robber peeled back his rubbery disguise
and powered his legs on Bopoluchi. A knock

at the door rocked him off for a knock-out deal.
He locked her indoors with his bald-headed mother
who dribbled her goofy chops at Bopoluchi's down-
to-her-feet braided mane! At once Bopoluchi put on
a simpleton's simper, professing her hair had grown

from its stubble with stipples from her mother's
pestle about her head in their rice-husking mortar.
When that bald-headed dreamer of long plaited hair
laid her head in a mortar her brains were bashed!
Bopoluchi arranged the body in her scarlet bridal dress
on a low bridal chair. The robber returned cock-a-hoop
and thought he saw Bopoluchi sat on a bridal chair.
Each time he bawled her name she bounced no reply.

He flipped his lid. He flung a mortar! Bopoluchi snuck
out the front as the robber blubbered into his beard
having eye-ball'd his twice-killed mummy-jee!
He went with his men to detect that slinky vixen.
Through the chink of a night they glimpsed her asleep
in the bed of her own audacious hut. And slithered in
like snakes to skilfully raise the bed by the legs
across a stream. When they reached the desert,

Bopoluchi, who all along had pretended to snore,
pulled ever so sweetly a snarling bill-hook. Swirling
its dervish screams she sliced off the goon-heads!
Except the robber who shot up a tree. Cried Bopoluchi,
You pukpukpuk chicken! Still he held to a branch
till she lit her stick-pile. Before heading for his house
on his horse to bag his pearls she purred when the food
that flew off the branch ready-made was roasted robber!

The Uncanny Cuteness of Being

We've been warned about you firstborns
but from day one you've dabbed your sister's cheek
and melted with *baby, ah baby* . . .

Still there's just no leaving you alone –
at night you'll doddle towards me
on the sofa-bed in your room.

I'm happy in here for this phase
now that 'mummy' paces our room
with our squirmy colicky *baby*.

Yet when my alarm startles
you snore to say this is where we part
so I'm left to sense your prod of toes

their candle glow on my back
for your second birthday.
Lifting your bottom

(with its soggy nappy) off my head
I snog the podge of your cheek
on my way for work.

The Knight

What, and chill with the drop-outs all spent on the park bench?
Old Toad, what a tease when you know I'm bound to
slave at the desk
so I'll summit the emerald mountain of Truth
on my knees as I drop my head
then buff with my dhoti the jewels on her shoes
as she swords me a CBE or an OBE or an MBE
or to someday arise through the depths Sir Dumdum Coolie!

Confessions of a Coolly Woman, Part I

I used each day to cushy sit and bag
    di rubber rings from belt at di factory,
den once at break a gora he cheeky
    chit-me-chat – wid tattoos am I stamped?
My heart it run to tell dat it not tattoo!
    It henna! From foot to hand it bloom
from life to life around my groom!
    My kismet bring me West to wed
    in caste so I not REJECT boxed!
And he? He add so sharp, he thorns is get
if he wrap himself round his Blighty rose!

One day his head it plopped to ground,
    his henna days, he chat, are stop now dat
his bride she take her bags for a man
    across di road. I add all goris are gund,
dey jaldi drop dey pants, dey freely foot
    and loose and fancy! He tink me potty
den joke vee binned in West to baddies –
    dey dump us home each night den *pant*
    wid dey bit on di side! In time vee bloom
our silly-billies – one day, he so confused:
vy all our lot get stuffed on Patak and

poppadum, tunking at night dey bongos?
    I also confused: vy all ju eat so much Oxo-
Paxo, tanning for Bingo, Disco? One break
    he buy me machine-made Tetley cup,
I say it tin, and pour from my flask
    masala tea but he, he say it tough
wid bits of cardamom, but still he drink!
    If looking in his eyes is touch,
    I touch him ven we learn to sit
wid our friend – di face ov Quiet – together
sipping our British or Indian cuppas . . .

Have I Got Old News for You

You've been mapping the best mortgage deals
for our first house, recalling the latest
tracker rate you hint we play it
safe with a five-year
fixed.

You're by the telly when Dubya flashes up,
he's happily in the past twitching his cowboy's
smirk on a mind-blowing thought
for smoking out them
Injuns!

I'm sorry Love, in the head to head, my head
had gone astray so you were second best,
it's just that I banked on a dead cert
gaffe to raise us
a laugh.

You don't hand me another Bud, but quiz my smiles
at this sniggery ad-lib game of gags
(that won your reddened
face back then).
I'm thrown

to those everyday courtship years in the clouds
with *Guantanamoww*, *Eyraaq*, and best
Affghanestaan liberated live
by our cream of suits:
John Simpsonian!

Octoroon

Ah sweet thing
with yellow curls & aqua eyes
the soapy bubbles that you blow
gasp at your cocoa skin.

I wonder do your True Blue parents
still force a
pompompomp
for The Last Night of the Proms?

The Punjab

Not 'The' – just 'Púnjab'!
Was there once upon before partition a Púnjab
whole? A Pan-jab of Hindu, Sikh, Muslim, anything?
Are Punjabis all partitioned? Are they puja pushers?
How many times was my punj-land picked off
so bank after river-bank got flagged by a clan?
To play the pipes of a Punjamentalist –
must I pin a badge, must I drop my pants –
must I join a junta and jab-jab-jab for my Púnjab!?

That old man river calls you loud and long
from a land that you loved in a lullaby

Yoo say 'Pún-jab' vee say Punjaaab –
it's our land of five wide rivers!
If it's five for the 'punj' and it's 'jaaab' for a river
so you'll never take me from
Ekjaab – Dohjaab – Tenjaab – Charjaab – Punjaaaaab!
What a jape! Not a jape, I'm the last of the line.
On the final day of my maa-baap I must palm
their ashes down the jaaab and watch them
panegyring to their 'Om'-land . . .

That old man river calls you loud and long
from a land that you loved in a lullaby
where the rainbow glows from a farm nearby

Do Púnjabs leave Punjaaab to spice the balti
of the W-W-W-World!? All I know is my people
deserted Punjab cos they're penny-puja pushers.
They sold me on the wind till I was anybody's
stand up Poppadum Pete cum Jalandhar Johnny.
But Ek-jaab is a row row your boat gently down the
swanny from Thames-jaab. Ah honey, let's bathe
in the waters of my ancestors
where you can pan at my jab or jaab for my man-jab!

That old man river calls you loud and long
from a land that you loved in a lullaby
where the rainbow glows from a farm nearby
but you'll never know the land or the song

Young Punglanders so many acres in the jaabland!
The jameen, the ghee, the jaggery or gor,
all those jagirs of gold in our names are ours
for the taking. I declare we're the pun of our maa-baap!
Take a pan & a lawman & jump aboard
for your unplucked jut-land, your bee-glade Indusfree!
Look at you jump! You golly well jump
my Huckleberry friend, look at you jumping
and jabbing your song down the jaabs going merrily –

Ekjaab-Dohjaab-Tenjaab-Charjaab-Punjaaaaaaaaaaaa ...

It's said two brows once ruled the roost & formed the global
look. In the way two legs or lips made a man complete
         two pert lines confirmed the Rule of Divide

when the West imposed its outlook about the hirsute belt
from Marrakech to outer Mongolia. What vision-empyrean
         in frescoes and oils from bold blue eyes!

Surely it's time, my dear, to review that vaunted gaze & bare
the single bushy brow. Evolution must be hedging for fusion
         if the eye-brow is the merger of humanity.

A child I was when the midriff I shaved
         before my kind I tottered a Victorian freak . . .

At the crown of my mammal-brow – an erectile ape-hair.
         Let's shed the burden of upright mankind.

True love deepens horizons with its temple over the eyes
         in the jungle of the hood! Each time we bed

into curried kisses feel my wonder-brow bursting against
         your stiff upper bald patch.

Slam!

Pow to the Max
 to my West-Skin Brown-Side clarion call
 4 u East End Rajas & Ranis!
Go wake yor inner brown beauty/
 How/How/Brown/How Brown/ Can u::::::::*Go!!!*

 I'm yor Gandhi at Zindabar Gate:
 drop yor jewels in the ring
 cum Mash up/Mash up their effffin'
 brown murdrin world
 enlightenin blaggerman word!

Don't lag with my rival Gang/Gang/Gangsta posers
 whose Hackney'd rap attack
 is a vocalizashun
 rhyme kondishun
 4 a foundashun-nashun!

Their socially-political in:yor:face lines
r dressed as poems cos they kill 2 b the wordSMITH!
But they come up against talk-2-the-hand

Romo-Greeko smartarse bumchums,
the twee, 'propa'

 (yawn

 yawn)

 Oxbrij

 P O W I T S!!!

The Legend of Lispeth

She would stare for her sahib-lover who'd gone
over the mountains of Kotgarh to his parents.
He claimed they lived in a neighbouring region,
and went alone to tell them his love for this girl
the Chaplain named after Queen Elizabeth,
thus dignifying her fusion of Penelope/Sita.
It took the Chaplain's wife to put her straight,

to help her regard her position; this baptised
orphan she and the Chaplain indulged
as their own flesh and blood (though inside
they knew she'd always be Indian!). At tiffin,
Lispeth heard the ladies: *A trumped-up child . . .*
Thinking that Blighty's across the way!
And above her station . . . with our men?

Dashing her cross to abandon their saviour,
she threw herself at the crags to be cleansed
of a name entire, of this Lispeth misnomer!
Then she roamed the heights with questions
about the way he'd duped her for sport.
Why, she wondered, had he strung her along
by leaving his butterfly expedition to flap

about her on the slopes of Narkunda with sonnets?
Or in the banyan shade was he that fascinated
by the noble aspects of English she displayed
that he mounted her Chaplain-reared side
for his private collection of exotic-beauties,
before his ablutions on a P&O liner
for his chaise longue'd Hampshire fiancée?

[38]

Did he think, she thinks, in the face to face
of the truth, at being informed it's over,
she'd be naturally wrought into force,
howling for alleys of furred men with sabres
to cauldron a fire, to fee-fie-foe
the heritage site of his gorgeous bones,
his delicious equanimous British blood?

Too dark now for the English for trying out
with a pure Christian, for the caste-bound
locals – too light, as wind banks on the cliffs
where she threads, re-threads her scraggly
mane and hears from across the poppy fields
bleating and mooing and tweeting as creatures
caution their own to keep from that cussed thing.

Father Figures

ROUND 1

When the Brits swaggered some ads
informing the gawping Punjabis
they could make a packet in the Motherland,
with Her Majesty dishing out
freebie travel vouchers,

the low castes, who loved Charlie Chaplin,
packed some rags on the end of a pole
and planked on to the next ocean liner.

Not one for nursing the puny rupee
he ditched his flip-flops and swung out
like Tarzan for the rock hard quid.

But he was lost in the Big Smoke.
And made to muck his hands with the head-lolling
paupers from home, over-timing from crud to cruddier job
where they knocked out stuff like rubber and Ready Brek.

ROUND 2

When he auditioned for professional wrestling
they ordered he be the baddie
barking at the ring-side biddies, he try to nobble
the ref or dropkick the stooled goodie-two-shoes rival
in the break between rounds. Then as rehearsed
he roll over – the loser to a blast of boos
before leaving the hall in a hissy fit.

He'd grappled in the milky sandpits and the drop dead
sun with the hardest lads known to man and won.
He was a curt fighter.
This handbags-at-dawn for infamy
floored him. He turned his back on wrestling.

ROUND 3

Your mum would push you into the room
when he'd call for you.
You'd be made to fight one of the older boys
of the men who'd gang round yours.

If you got beaten you'd have to stand for his trivia.
The air ripe with the smell of munched green chillies
when he'd ask you to spell out words like lieutenant
(he'd say it with a 'f'). Or weirdly he'd count down
while you'd have to name animals in Punjabi.

He was a whippy quiz master who left you muddle-headed.
He'd call you a sher. You knew this meant tiger.
And knew what he meant when you'd watch the men,
drowning in bottles of Johnnie Walker,
wail their laughs and throw up claps.

ROUND 4

Upside-down with his bull-neck
and bald-headed palm-handed dance
on the petals and stems of the red carpet –

he'd take your breath
in the grand-as-possible knocked-through lounge
of your three-bed semi. Mum's knitting needles

clacking their jumper joy
for The Champion Heavyweight of Hindustan
who didn't sell out and wrestle on *Grandstand*.

You loved it when he came home legless
from The Six Bells
in his dentedly driven Mustang.
You'd plead him into one-armed press-ups –
he'd clown out, with claps in-between, ten on the spot!

Or lifting a chair by the base of the leg
he'd juggle it cleanly between arms
but the best was when he watched you swoon

at his handstand-feet hanging trapeze
as pennies tumbled from his pockets!

Dance of the Cosmic Brew

Ootle-tootle
on a sunny day like today

what can I say but hoot for the
toot. Let's settle down for a loos-
ened brew & mourn the golden age
when a teapot adorned a body of tiger & dragon spout.
Just then you saunter off the patio & become a teapot
doing a kooky spout dance to hoot-hoots & toots!
O *Madhu*, I say, *I'm yours to the ends.*
O *Sadhu*, you say, *the earth's first*
flush is in the tips of our tips . . .
Our whirling arms are swirls
from Saturn, we're teapot
helicopter

punkah-doctors in our garden going:
hoot-hoot, rootle-tootle, ootle-tootle-tootle!

Kabbadi *Keeegun!!!*

On one breath allowed
(proved by chanting *kabbadi*)
he runs inside from the line
for an arc of Walsall's defenders –
with a lunge he touches a limb,
the defender must break to pin him
out of his breath, but that's a dream
as my uncle's already turning
and turned shimmying for the centre.

With our granddads and dads, us fans
of Southall invade waving
fivers and tenners – slapped
on his oil'd chest or laid at his feet,
cos he's the raider who scored
the trophy point, against his pleas
he's raised through the crowd to the sun
and compared by chants to his hero:
Keeegun!!! Keeegun!!! Keeegun!!!

In class, I'd go with the chat of
Keegan winning the European Cup
or Golden Boot with Hamburg
hitting the charts with 'Head over
Heels', but I'd keep *our* Keegan
and the ways of our world
to myself or I'd be knocked
into touch
by lads up for footie alone.

This fatherless boat-boy, a packer
at Walls (who sleeps on *my* floor!),
inherited debts to the family,
yet he was the Captain of England
touring the globe on unpaid leave.
Behind his back, while he's at his
peak, my parents hounding
marriage-brokers to win us
the finest figure.

Retired to Mansfield as part
of the deal, he runs a cousin's store.
Though once in a while he's forced
after thugs who escape in cars
he'll chase round the bend as they
chuck dribbling cans at his feet
impressed by the man they've heard
will follow them over the rise
with the ends of the sun on his back.

The Constant Art

It's true my love's a paid up fashion victim.

Her hair, for a start, each morn is blandly ironed
glossy down her back; her nails are on nails
(embedded with gems) though when in heated kiss
they'll sometimes stay there hanging in my neck.

Yet she's no bendu dumbo reared on farms
to wrestle bulls, her battle's with tash and arms
she'll wax; but when I see her cut by friends
for wearing last year's cut, I think of times
I've worn my heart at sleeve and that's not *cool*.

O love, these things are forging fickle youth!

Let's drop our guard for goods that rarely lie,
monuments like sonnets that will age
their solid lines in us to save our face.

'Look there he goes even now, my father'

Look there he goes even now, my father,
into some other world, all my life
I have been harbour-struck
trying to make him appear
from wherever he went
the years before
I was born . . .

Ken

(15/09/24 – 10/08/09)

We visit your granddad down
  at Land's End, at your auntie's
    mill he's throned on a fireside
      plum-leather seat. Having swallowed
     the chore of his morning drugs
    he waffs on a peppermint tea
   then sinks back in himself.

My kin believe the old
  must spin out bygone yarns
    to keep in the light. Ken rapidly
     rattles the daily John Bull
    yarns of his doolally pilot
   years; to sense his mind's
    sparked I invite him to cite

the lit, you say, he learned
  by rote at grammar school.
    He goes *Out out* then stalls
     and dodders a Kitchener finger.
    You watch me turn to the 'net
   to find him his Bard's lines,
    but sudden a winging

fist and raggedy voice
   flicker alert from nowhere:
      Out, out brief candle –
         life's but a walking shadow,
            a poor player . . . And on
               till we applaud and place
                  on his legs his favoured blanket.

I've heard that my illiterate
   granddad, a turbaned warrior
      turned hobbler who stayed back home,
         spent his days on a courtyard
            charpoy summoning battle
               ballads with only the cows
                  and the clap-along village idiot.

A Black History of the English-Speaking Peoples

I

A king's invocations at the Globe Theatre
spin me from my stand to a time when boyish
        bravado and cannonade
and plunder were enough to woo the regal seat.

That the stuff of Elizabethan art and a nation
of walled gardens in a local one-up manship
        would tame the four-cornered
world for Empire's dominion seems inconceivable.

Between the birth and the fire and rebirth of the Globe
the visions of Albion led to a Rule Britannia
        of trade-winds-and-Gulf-Stream
all-conquering fleets that aroused theatres

for lectures on Hottentots and craniology,
whilst Eden was paraded in Kew.
        Between *Mayflower* and *Windrush*
(with each *necessary murder*) the celebrated

embeddings of imperial gusto where jungles
were surmounted so the light of learning be spread
        to help sobbing suttees
give up the ghost of a husband's flaming pyre.

II

So much for yesterday, but today's time-honoured
televised clashes repeat the flag of a book burning
        and May Day's Mohican
Churchill and all that shock and awe

that brings me back to Mr Wanamaker's Globe.
An American's thatched throwback to the king
        of the canon! I watch the actor
as king, from the cast of masterful Robeson.

The crowd, too, seem a hotchpotch from the pacts
and sects of our ebb and flow. My forbears played
        their part for the Empire's quid
pro quo by assisting the rule and divide of their ilk.

Did such relations bear me to this stage?
Especially with Macaulay in mind, who claimed the passing
        of the imperial sceptre would highlight
the imperishable empire of our arts . . .

So does the red of Macaulay's map run through
my blood? Am I a noble scruff who hopes a proud
        academy might canonise
his poems for their faith·in canonical allusions?

Is my voice phoney over these oft-heard beats?
Well if my voice feels vexatious, what can I but pray
        that it reign Bolshie
through puppetry and hypocrisy full of gung-ho fury!

III

The heyday Globe incited brave new verse
modelled on the past, where time's frictions
        courted Shakespeare's corruptions
for tongue's mastery of the pageant subject. Perhaps

the Globe should be my muse! I'm happy digging
for my England's good garden to bear again.
        My garden's only a state
of mind, where it's easy aligning myself with a 'turncoat'

T. E. Lawrence and a *half-naked fakir* and always
the groundling. Perhaps to aid the succession
        of this language of the world,
for the poet weeding the roots, for the debate

in ourselves, now we're bound to the wheels
of global power, we should tend the manorial
        slime – that legacy
offending the outcasts who fringe our circles.

IV

Who believes a bleached yarn? Would we openly
admit the Livingstone spirit turned Kurtz, our flag
        is a union of black and blue
flapping in the anthems of haunted rain . . . ?

Coming clean would surely give us greater distance
than this king at the Globe, whose head seems cluttered
        with golden-age bumph,
whose suffering ends him agog at the stars.

v

I applaud and stroll toward Westminster,
yet softly tonight the waters of Britannia bobble
        with flotillas of tea and white gold
cotton and sugar and the sweetness-and-light

blood lettings and ultimately red-faced Suez.
And how swiftly the tide removes from the scene
        the bagpipe clamouring
garrisons with the field-wide scarlet soldiery

and the martyr's cry: *Every man die at his post!*
Till what's ahead are the upbeat lovers who gaze
        from the London Eye
at multinationals lying along the sanitised Thames.

Bolly Bhaji

Banchudes – replace 'mum' with 'sister' in 'yer mum!'
bendu – villager
Bettychudes – replace 'mum' with 'daughter' in 'yer mum!'
bezti – disgraceful!
bobbery – noisy
Bolly – language
burra – whopper
coolly – loose (morally or materially)
cushy – happy
dooshman – foe
fettlin' – (Yorkshire Punjabi) cleanin'
goodies – girls
gori – white babe
gund – dirt (morally or materially)
gunna, gor – cane sugar
haar – (usually) a gaudy tinsel garland
Hobson-Jobsons – 'native festal excitement[s]'
   (from Hobson Jobson)
jagirs – estates
jameen – land
jut – landowner caste
lungar – freebie gurdwara food
matyai – sweets such as barfi, chum-chum, gujrelaaa . . .
nautch – 'ballet-dance performed by women'
   (from Hobson Jobson)
pawnee – water
Rub – GOD!
sharam – bezti
shikar – a jolly good hunt
zenana – where the women are kept